W9-CKI-769

MILWAUKEE
BREWERS

by Gary Derong

SportsZone

An Imprint of Abdo Publishing
www.abdopublishing.com

www.abdopublishing.com

Published by Abdo Publishing, a division of ABDO, PO Box 398166, Minneapolis, Minnesota 55439. Copyright © 2015 by Abdo Consulting Group, Inc. International copyrights reserved in all countries. No part of this book may be reproduced in any form without written permission from the publisher. SportsZone is a trademark and logo of Abdo Publishing.

Printed in the United States of America, North Mankato, Minnesota
052014
092014

THIS BOOK CONTAINS
RECYCLED MATERIALS

Editor: Matt Tustison
Copy Editor: Nicholas Cafarelli
Interior Design and Production: Carol Castro
Cover Design: Craig Hinton

Photo Credits: Jeff Curry/AP Images, cover; AP Images, title, 7, 12, 14, 16, 18, 21, 22, 25, 42 (top and middle); Steve Pyle/AP Images, 9, 31, 42 (bottom), 43 (top); Getty Images, 11, 32; Photo by Bernstein Associates/Getty Images, 26; John Swart/AP Images, 29; Charles Tasnadi/AP Images, 34; Andy Manis/AP Images, 37, 43 (middle); Morry Gash/AP Images, 39, 40, 43 (bottom), 47; Ronald C. Modra/Sports Imagery/Getty Images, 44

Library of Congress Control Number: 2014933082
Cataloging-in-Publication Data
Derong, Gary, 1950-
  Milwaukee Brewers / by Gary Derong.
      p. cm. — (Inside MLB)
  Includes bibliographical references and index.
  ISBN 978-1-62403-475-6
  1. Milwaukee Brewers (Baseball team)—History—Juvenile Literature. I. Title.
  GV875.M53D47 2015
  796.357'640977595—dc23
                        2014933082

TABLE OF CONTENTS

CHAPTER 1

A SEASON TO REMEMBER

T

he most promising season in Milwaukee Brewers history was crashing.

The Brewers needed only one victory in a four-game series at Baltimore to clinch the 1982 American League (AL) East title. But the Orioles won the first three games. In those games, the Brewers were outscored by a combined 26–7.

The season came down to its final game. The Brewers had never won a division title. The Orioles, on the other hand, were

Power to Spare

Three Brewers hit more than 30 home runs in 1982. Gorman Thomas slugged 39, Ben Oglivie added 34, and Cecil Cooper contributed 32. As a team, the Brewers hit 216 homers, the most in baseball since 1964. They also led the majors in runs scored with 891, runs batted in (RBIs) with 843, total bases with 2,606, and slugging percentage at .455. "It was contagious," said Robin Yount, who led the AL in hits, total bases, slugging percentage, and doubles while batting .331 with 29 homers and 114 RBIs.

Veteran Don Sutton came through for Milwaukee in 1982. His strong pitching helped the team win 10–2 at Baltimore in the season finale to clinch the AL East title.

MANAGERIAL CHANGES

The Brewers switched managers twice during the most successful period in their history.

The team thought George Bamberger would be in charge for many years after he led Milwaukee to 93 victories in 1978. But Bamberger, whose slugging Brewers became known as "Bambi's Bombers," suffered a heart attack that caused him to miss some of the 1980 season. He resigned after that season. Bob "Buck" Rodgers, the team's third-base coach, replaced him. Rodgers led the Brewers to their first postseason appearance. They lost to the New York Yankees.

The next year, longtime team hitting coach Harvey Kuenn replaced Rodgers as manager. The players loved Kuenn, who lost his right leg to a blood circulation problem in 1980. Under Kuenn, the Brewers quickly regained their winning ways as "Harvey's Wallbangers."

used to playing in the postseason and winning the World Series. Baltimore pitched its ace, Jim Palmer. Milwaukee started Don Sutton, a former Los Angeles Dodgers star nearing the end of his career.

Manager Harvey Kuenn showed his faith in his pitcher. "I'm going to cross my good leg over my bad leg, sit in my corner of the dugout, and watch an old pro go to work," said Kuenn, who had an artificial leg.

Sutton did his part, out-pitching Palmer. Shortstop Robin Yount, a budding superstar, also did his. He hit two homers and a triple as Milwaukee won 10–2. The Brewers finally had a championship to celebrate.

But more tension followed in the postseason. By the time the Brewers played their first home game in the

The Brewers' Pete Vuckovich lets go of a pitch in 1982. Vuckovich finished the season 18–6 with a 3.34 ERA and won the AL Cy Young Award.

best-of-five AL Championship Series (ALCS), they were on the verge of being eliminated. The California Angels won the first two games in Anaheim 8–3 and 4–2. So the Brewers had to win three straight at Milwaukee County Stadium to claim their first World Series berth. Sutton pitched them to a 5–3 victory in Game 3. Then the Brewers won Game 4 9–5.

Game 5 was winner take all, with the pennant at stake. The crowd was on the Brewers' side. But the Angels were a team with many postseason veterans.

Milwaukee entered the late innings trailing 3–2. A bloop hit

PRECIOUS PITCHERS

Harry Dalton earned a special place among Brewers general managers with two trades.

The biggest one, made after the 1980 season, brought the next two AL Cy Young Award winners to Milwaukee. Dalton sent outfielder Sixto Lezcano and three other players to St. Louis. In return, the Brewers got all-star catcher Ted Simmons and pitchers Rollie Fingers and Pete Vuckovich. Fingers, the Brewers' closer, won the Cy Young Award in 1981 as the league's best pitcher. Vuckovich anchored the starting staff and won the Cy Young in 1982.

Dalton traded for another big-game starting pitcher to go with Vuckovich and Mike Caldwell on August 30, 1982, when he sent young outfielder Kevin Bass and two lesser players to Houston for future Hall of Famer Don Sutton.

by Charlie Moore, however, got the Brewers started in the seventh. Jim Gantner followed with a sharp single. After Paul Molitor popped out, Yount walked to load the bases. Cecil Cooper then delivered Milwaukee's biggest postseason hit. His opposite-field single to left scored Moore and Gantner.

But the 4–3 victory was not completed until rookie relief pitcher Pete Ladd retired Rod Carew, a seven-time AL batting champion. Carew hit a sharp one-hopper to Yount at shortstop. Yount made the throw to Cooper at first base. The Brewers erupted. A World Series date with the St. Louis Cardinals awaited.

Game 1 could not have gone any better for the Brewers. Mike Caldwell hushed the crowd in St. Louis with his baffling sinkerball. His teammates pounded out 17 hits and

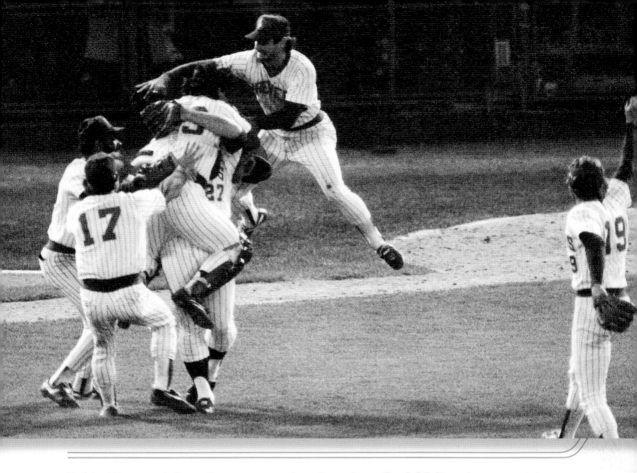

Robin Yount, *right*, raises an arm in triumph as Paul Molitor leaps to join teammates in celebrating the Brewers' 1982 ALCS series victory.

10 runs. Molitor set a World Series single-game record with five hits. Yount added four in the 10–0 rout.

All but one of the other Series games were tense. After the Brewers earned 7–5 and 6–4 victories, they led the Series three games to two heading to St. Louis. But the Cardinals halted the Brewers' momentum in Game 6. St. Louis built an 8–0 lead. The Cardinals then added five more runs after a long rain delay for a 13–1 rout.

Another winner-take-all game awaited the Brewers. Cy Young Award winner

Pete Vuckovich held Milwaukee in the game for five innings. But it was not long enough. The Cardinals made up a 3–1 deficit by scoring three in the sixth and two in the eighth against the Brewers' worn-out bullpen. St. Louis won the game 6–3 and the World Series four games to three.

Milwaukee blamed its World Series loss on the elbow injury that ended closer Rollie Fingers's season in early September. The future Hall of Famer with the handlebar mustache was the AL Most Valuable Player (MVP) and the Cy Young Award winner in 1981.

But despite Milwaukee's defeat in the World Series, TV viewers nationwide were charmed by this offbeat team of "Wallbangers." Being a Brewers fan suddenly became cool. And that was quite a change for an unloved team that had gone bankrupt and was moved after its first year of existence.

One Last Roar

Losing the last two games of the World Series left the Brewers in no mood to celebrate. But Milwaukee wanted to say thank you to the team. A downtown parade and rally at County Stadium were arranged. In front of about 20,000 fans, the players walked onto the field as they were individually introduced. When Robin Yount's name was called, he was nowhere to be seen. Then the bullpen gate opened way out in right-center field, and out onto the field roared a motorcycle whose rider was dressed in leather. It was Yount, the soon-to-be-named AL MVP. "I was just kind of being a rebel or whatever," he said. The crowd loved it.

The Brewers' Cecil Cooper follows through on his swing as Cardinals catcher Darrell Porter looks on during Game 4 of the 1982 World Series. Milwaukee won 7–5 that day but lost the series in seven games.

CHAPTER 2

BEGGAR BUD

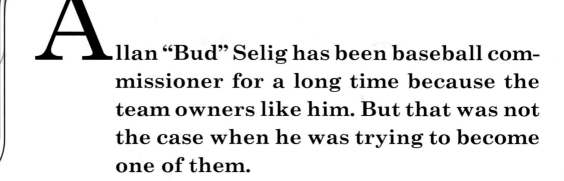

Allan "Bud" Selig has been baseball commissioner for a long time because the team owners like him. But that was not the case when he was trying to become one of them.

As the leader of a Milwaukee group trying to land a team in the late 1960s, he was an unwelcome guest at owners meetings. He often could be found lurking in the lobby of the owners' hotel. "We'd look behind a potted palm, and there would be Buddy," said Buzzie Bavasi, a former big-league executive.

At one meeting, AL president Joe Cronin looked at Selig

Near Miss

The Chicago White Sox were struggling to draw fans when they struck a deal to play nine home games at County Stadium in 1968 and 11 more in 1969. The games in Milwaukee drew larger crowds than the White Sox were getting at Comiskey Park, so Bud Selig tried to buy the team from owners John and Arthur Allyn Jr. to move it to Milwaukee. He said he made a handshake deal with Arthur Allyn, but John Allyn said no. The dispute was settled with Arthur Allyn selling his interest in the Sox to his younger brother.

Bud Selig reads a telegram on April 1, 1970. The telegram said the Seattle Pilots had declared bankruptcy. The team would soon move to Milwaukee and be renamed the Brewers. Selig would be the new owner.

Catcher Jerry McNertney is shown in 1969 with the Seattle Pilots. The Pilots existed for just that one season before moving to Milwaukee and becoming the Brewers.

and asked, "What are you doing here again?"

Owners did not dislike Selig as much as they did Milwaukee. "Baseball didn't want to come back here under any circumstances," Selig said.

"We'd go to baseball meetings, and we were treated like we had leprosy."

Milwaukee had been the Braves' home beginning in 1953, after the National League (NL) team had moved from

Boston. But the Braves moved to Atlanta after the 1965 season. The Braves' owners wanted to leave a year earlier. A ruling by a Milwaukee judge, however, forced them to keep the team in Milwaukee in 1965. The other teams' owners were bitter. They saw better places to put a new team than Milwaukee. After all, the city was practically in Chicago's backyard at only 90 miles (145 km) away.

It Pays to Recycle

"Brewers" was an easy choice for the team's nickname because Milwaukee was famous for brewing beer and because the nickname was used as far back as 1901. The 1901 Milwaukee Brewers were an AL team that moved to St. Louis after only one year and became the Browns. The Browns moved to Baltimore after the 1953 season and became the Orioles. Milwaukee also had a minor league team called the Brewers in the Triple-A American Association before the Braves arrived from Boston in 1953.

Milwaukee's last hope of regaining a team rested with another judge. The Seattle Pilots of the AL were having problems paying their bills after only one season of operation. Selig's group was pursuing the Pilots. Milwaukee County Stadium, the former home of the Braves, would become the Pilots' new home. But first a Seattle judge had to declare the team bankrupt.

The Pilots went to Tempe, Arizona, for spring training in 1970. They did not know where they would call home during the season. With spring training almost over, their equipment trucks drove north to Las Vegas and waited.

The ruling of bankruptcy came on April 1. It was no April Fools' joke—although the team could pass for one. The Pilots had little talent and few recognizable names. But on

April 5, they landed at Milwaukee's airport and were treated like heroes by a gathering of baseball fans.

"It was unbelievable," first baseman Mike Hegan said. "There was never that kind of interest in Seattle. We were kind of shocked. None of us knew anything about Milwaukee. When we got to the airport, people were there with signs, ready to greet us."

Two days later, 37,237 fans at County Stadium watched the team take the field as the Brewers. Letters that formed the word Pilots had been ripped off the uniforms and replaced with Brewers. After a 12–0 pasting by the California Angels, Milwaukee residents were saying, "We wanted baseball back in the worst way, and that's what we got." The joke lasted for most of the 1970s.

The Original Bernie

Bernie Brewer is known today as a mascot who goes down a slide to celebrate Brewers home runs. But the original Bernie made one slide down a rope, and, boy, did that hurt. In 1970, Milt Mason agreed to live on top of the County Stadium scoreboard from July 6 until there was a sellout crowd. A trailer was installed, and Mason came out on a platform to watch the games. He called himself "Bernie Brewer." But the losing team still was not drawing big crowds. So Bernie lowered his goal to a crowd of 40,000. "Bat Day" on August 16 drew 44,387, and Bernie was freed. But instead of using the steps to go down the scoreboard, he requested a rope to make a more dramatic return to Earth. The 69-year-old retired man slid down the rope so fast he bloodied his hands. "It was a great experience, but I wouldn't do it again," he said.

The Atlanta Braves' Hank Aaron signs autographs in Milwaukee on May 14, 1970. The Braves and the Brewers played an exhibition that day. Aaron had been a star with the Milwaukee Braves before the team moved to Atlanta.

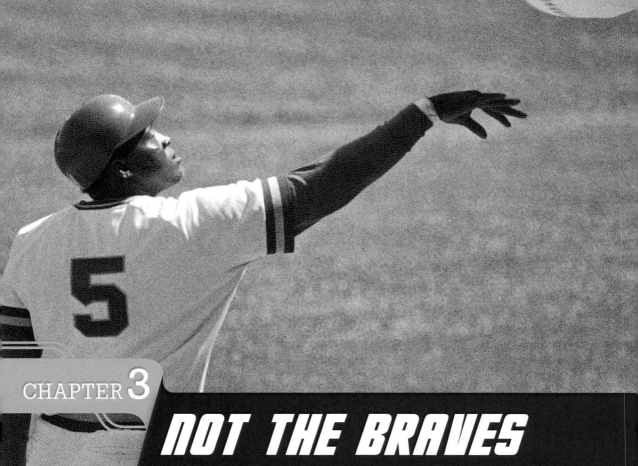

CHAPTER 3

NOT THE BRAVES

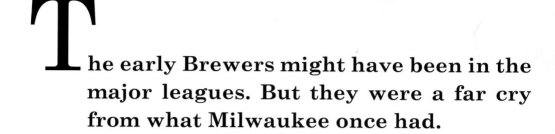

The early Brewers might have been in the major leagues. But they were a far cry from what Milwaukee once had.

The Milwaukee Braves were instantly lovable. In 1953, they won their first home game on a dramatic 10th-inning home run. They beat the mighty New York Yankees for the 1957 World Series championship. They fell just short of repeating against the Yankees in the 1958 Series. The NL team never had a losing season during its 13 years in America's Dairyland.

"Milwaukee Miracle"

Boston Braves owner Lou Perini announced on March 13, 1953, that he planned to move his team to Milwaukee. The Braves drew only 281,278 fans in 1952 while sharing Boston with the more successful Red Sox. But in their first season as the Milwaukee Braves, they attracted more than 1.8 million, an NL record. And 1954 began a streak of four consecutive seasons in which the Braves drew more than 2 million. Baseball officials called that period the "Milwaukee Miracle."

First baseman George Scott throws an inflatable baseball back into the stands in Milwaukee in 1976. The Brewers struggled during their first several seasons. Many fans were still angry that the Braves had left town.

MR. BASEBALL

Bob Uecker was a Milwaukee native and a former backup catcher for his hometown Braves. In 1970, he asked Bud Selig for a job with the Brewers. Selig suggested that he scout minor league players. But one day, Selig received a scouting report turned in by Uecker. Stains from mashed potatoes and gravy had made it unreadable. "I knew then that he wasn't going to make it as a scout, so we decided to try him as a broadcaster," Selig said.

That raw radio color man in 1971 became a baseball broadcasting Hall of Famer in 2003. Uecker's ability to tell funny stories kept fans listening to games. It also turned Uecker into a national celebrity. His many appearances on *The Tonight Show* earned Uecker the nickname of "Mr. Baseball" from Johnny Carson. A part-time acting career followed, including a memorable role as Cleveland Indians radio broadcaster Harry Doyle in the movie *Major League*.

Future Hall of Famers Eddie Mathews and Hank Aaron formed a powerful heart of the Braves' batting order. Future Hall of Famer Warren Spahn and Lew Burdette led the talented pitching staff.

The Braves helped change baseball's landscape with their success. A year after the Braves' 1953 move from Boston, the St. Louis Browns moved to Baltimore and became the Orioles. A year after that, the Philadelphia Athletics moved to Kansas City. In 1958, the Dodgers moved from Brooklyn to Los Angeles and the Giants from New York to San Francisco. But Milwaukee saw this trend's other side when the Braves left for Atlanta after the 1965 season. Many Braves fans vowed never to set foot in County Stadium again. The arrival in 1970 of a bumbling

Outfielder Hank Aaron is shown in 1954, when he was a rookie with the Milwaukee Braves. Aaron led the Braves to a World Series title in 1957.

expansion team that played in the "other league" made it easy for many of those Braves diehards to keep their word.

"The first few years were a struggle," Brewers owner Bud Selig said. "One thing I miscalculated was the anger and bitterness over the Braves leaving. It was really deep."

Two things happened in 1974 to connect the Brewers with Wisconsin baseball fans. The first was the arrival of a potential superstar. The second was the homecoming of

Robin Yount watches a ball he hit in 1974. Yount was the Brewers' starting shortstop that season as an 18-year-old rookie.

baseball's newly crowned home-run king.

Robin Yount, meet Henry Aaron.

The woeful Brewers had nothing to lose when they inserted Yount into the Opening Day lineup in 1974. Yount was a gangly 18-year-old shortstop prospect. His lack of experience showed on defense. He committed 19 errors in his injury-shortened rookie year and a whopping 44 in 1975. But he rewarded the Brewers' patience. Yount went on to become the first player to win AL MVP Awards at two positions. He achieved Hall of Fame status for a 20-year career spent entirely with Milwaukee.

Twenty years before Yount came on the scene, rookie Hank Aaron debuted at County Stadium in 1954 for the Milwaukee Braves. Three years later, Aaron won the NL MVP Award and hit a pennant-clinching home run in the 11th inning on September 23 against the visiting St. Louis Cardinals. He was carried off the field by his teammates. A World Series championship over the Yankees then put Aaron and Milwaukee on top of the baseball world.

"Hammerin' Hank" became an even bigger home-run threat in an Atlanta Braves stadium known as "the Launching Pad." In 1974, he received worldwide attention as he drew close to the major league career home-run record. The mark was held by the legendary Babe Ruth. Aaron passed Ruth by hitting number 715 on April 8 against Los Angeles Dodgers pitcher Al Downing. The scene at Atlanta-Fulton County Stadium was raucous.

But the fact that Ruth was white and Aaron was an African American had created an ugly tension to the home-run chase.

"Boomer"

First baseman George "Boomer" Scott, a Brewer from 1972 to 1976, was a team leader like no other. He was strong and headstrong. He held court among the players and collected fines from those he judged to have messed up on the field. He once challenged an opposing manager to a fight when he thought that team's pitchers were throwing at him and his teammates. He had his own vocabulary and called home runs "taters." And he could play. In 1975, he tied for the AL home-run title with 36 and led the league with 109 RBIs. He also won his seventh Gold Glove Award.

Aaron received death threats before breaking Ruth's record. He said he did not feel the love in Atlanta that he felt in Milwaukee. So, he welcomed the news in November 1974 that the Braves had traded him to the Brewers. Atlanta received outfielder Dave May and minor league pitcher Roger Alexander in exchange.

Aaron's return to Milwaukee and the city's buildup to the 1975 All-Star Game at County Stadium breathed life into the Brewers. But Aaron was just a shadow of the player who had played right field for the Milwaukee Braves. Even in the less-strenuous role of designated hitter, he batted only .234 with 12 homers and 60 RBIs in 1975. He played less often in 1976. In fact, his 10th and last homer—number 755 of his career—came not in September but on July 20.

But Selig never regretted trading for Aaron. His presence in the Brewers' lineup helped the team set an attendance record of 1.2 million in 1975. Included in that total was a turnout of 48,160 on a very cold April 11 for "Welcome Home, Henry Day."

Aaron said: "I'll never forget walking out on that County Stadium field, the same field my teammates had carried me off when we won the pennant

Hank Aaron poses in 1975. The Brewers' acquisition of baseball's all-time home-run king before that season helped spark interest in the team.

in 1957, and hearing those fans screaming and singing for me. It made me realize how much I'd missed that place."

Aaron's time with the Brewers was short and unproductive. But he received the ultimate thank you for all he did for Milwaukee by having his No. 44 retired by the Brewers. But those who had dreamt of Aaron teaming up with Yount to turn the Brewers into contenders were disappointed. Yount would have to wait until 1978 to get such a partner. His name was Paul Molitor.

CHAPTER 4

MOLLY AND "THE KID"

Robin Yount beat Paul Molitor to the major leagues by four years. But Yount is only 11 months older than Molitor. Known for most of his career as "The Kid," Yount was drafted by Milwaukee out of high school. Molitor had a successful college career at the University of Minnesota before turning pro.

"You could tell he was going to be a star," Brewers scout Dee Fondy said of Molitor. Molitor was the third overall pick in the 1977 draft, just as Yount had been in 1973. Like Yount, Molitor played in only 64 minor league games and was the Brewers' Opening Day shortstop the following year. Molitor was a replacement in 1978 for Yount, who was hurt.

But the reverse situation was more common. Injuries hampered Molitor early in his career. They included torn ligaments in his ankle that required surgery and two operations on

Paul Molitor waits in the on-deck circle as longtime Brewers teammate Robin Yount bats against the Angels in 1992.

his right elbow. As a result, Molitor missed many games.

"In my mind, if Paulie hadn't gotten hurt so much, I think he would have been able to catch Pete Rose for total hits," said Gorman Thomas, a former Brewer. Rose holds the major league record with 4,256 hits in his career.

When healthy, the man known to his teammates as "Molly" was Yount's equal in terms of combining speed, power, and baseball smarts. "He's a Rod Carew with power" is the way Yount described him. As the Brewers' leadoff hitter, Molitor stole 41 bases and scored 136 runs in the World Series season of 1982.

In 1987, Molitor had the spotlight all to himself as he approached one of baseball's most famous records: Joe DiMaggio's 56-game hitting streak. Molitor started a 39-game streak on July 16. It was the day he came off the disabled list after spending 19 days on it because of a hamstring

"Gumby" Makes Three

In 1978, the same year Paul Molitor debuted for the Brewers, a 12th-round draft choice from tiny Eden, Wisconsin, made the team as a utility infielder. Jim Gantner had nowhere near the Hall of Fame talent of Molitor or Robin Yount. Nevertheless, those three players would go on to play 15 years together in Milwaukee. That was the longest association of three teammates in major league history until the New York Yankees' Derek Jeter, Mariano Rivera, and Jorge Posada passed them in 2010. "He was funny without trying to be funny," Yount said of "Gumby," who did not always use the English language correctly but was a model of consistency on the field.

Milwaukee players, including Robin Yount (19), celebrate on April 20, 1987. The Brewers had just beaten the host White Sox 5–4 to improve to 13–0.

injury. Molitor did not seriously threaten DiMaggio's mark. But he helped bring national attention to Milwaukee after a five-year quiet period. "Looking back, it was a lot of fun," said Molitor, who showed he could be comfortable alone on a big stage.

He shared the big stage with his teammates at the start of that 1987 season. Under first-year manager Tom Trebelhorn, Milwaukee rocketed out of the starting gate. The Brewers piled up victory after victory. Coming off a 77–84 season in 1986, Milwaukee was the surprise of baseball. The Brewers' 13 straight victories set an AL record for a season-opening winning streak.

But the joy of April was followed by sadness in May. Milwaukee lost 12 in a row that month. The seeing-eye hits that contributed to the Brewers'

success in April were nowhere to be found in May. Adding to Milwaukee's downturn was the loss of Molitor to his hamstring injury in June.

The Brewers, however, righted themselves after the All-Star break behind Molitor's hitting onslaught and Teddy Higuera's pitching. Milwaukee finished the 1987 season in third place in the AL East, seven games out of first, with a 91–71 record. On the night Molitor's 39-game hitting streak

The Spoiler

Paul Molitor's 39-game hitting streak ended with Molitor standing in the on-deck circle at County Stadium and a crowd of 11,246 booing the game-winning single that pinch-hitter Rick Manning delivered in the 10th inning of a 1–0 victory over Cleveland on August 26, 1987. Molitor was the first player to greet and congratulate Manning for the hit. "I went up to him, and he said, 'Sorry,'" Molitor recalled. "I said: 'Sorry? You just won the game.'"

Paul Molitor connects for a sixth-inning single on August 25, 1987, against the Indians to extend his hitting streak to 39 games.

was snapped, Higuera started a scoreless-innings streak that reached a team-record 32 innings. Is it any wonder that the 1987 Brewers were called "Team Streak"?

Milwaukee played mostly solid baseball for the next several seasons. The Brewers finished with records of .500 or better in 1988, 1989, and 1991. But it was not until 1992 that the team got back to the 90-win plateau.

Molitor and Yount had grown used to playing for power-hitting Brewers teams. That changed in 1992 under new

Pat Listach runs during the 1992 season. Listach, who would be chosen AL Rookie of the Year, was part of a speedy Brewers team that competed for the AL East title.

manager Phil Garner. Garner, known as "Scrap Iron," spent most of his 16-year playing career in the NL. That league emphasizes running, bunting, and manufacturing runs more than the AL, which has the designated hitter.

Scrappy NL ball came to Milwaukee in a big way in 1992. Garner not only had the base-running ability of Molitor and Yount to lean on. But he also had two other fast players in rookie shortstop Pat Listach and young center fielder

Darryl Hamilton. "We didn't have a home run-hitting club," Garner said. "We had to score runs doing things differently. . . . We ran randomly."

Listach became the AL Rookie of the Year after stealing a team-record 54 bases in 1992. Hamilton swiped 41. In all, the Brewers made off with 256. This was almost 100 more than the AL's next-best team.

Surprisingly, Milwaukee also led the league in pitching, with a 3.43 earned-run average (ERA), and in defense, with a .986 fielding percentage. This again mimicked the NL style of play. Garner's team stayed in the AL East race until the second-to-last day of the season.

The Toronto Blue Jays were the new power in the East. But the Brewers (92–70) were competitive and exciting under Garner. So, why was there not much optimism heading into 1993? It was because the gap between rich and poorer teams in baseball was widening. Milwaukee general manager Sal Bando had been ordered to trim payroll. Brewers fans noticed that their team had been unable to add a key player or two for the 1992 division race. Things would only get worse.

They did in December 1992. That month, Molitor was allowed to leave Milwaukee as a free agent. He signed a three-year, $13 million contract with rival Toronto.

Molitor would lead the Blue Jays to the 1993 World Series championship as the Series MVP, later collect his 3,000th hit as a member of his hometown Minnesota Twins, and join Yount in the Hall of Fame.

The Brewers would not have another winning season until 2007.

CHAPTER 5

BIG CHANGES

500·9911

Even "The Kid" got old. Robin Yount played a last-place 1993 season without Paul Molitor at his side before calling it a career. The Brewers were entering a period in which bigger stories occurred off the field than on it.

Bud Selig became baseball's acting commissioner on September 9, 1992—the day Yount collected his 3,000th career hit. Team owners ousted the previous commissioner, Fay Vincent.

As commissioner, Selig helped to give more teams hope by expanding the playoffs to include a wild-card team in each league. This forced a realignment in 1994. Each league went from two divisions

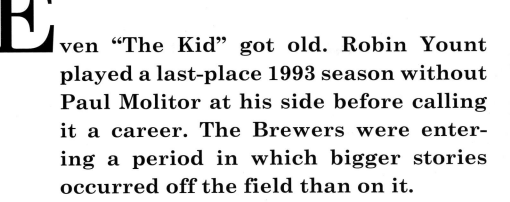

Stay-at-Home Czar

Commissioner Bud Selig moved baseball's operations center from New York to Milwaukee. Although his role changed from team owner to the most important person in baseball, his daily habits did not. Customers in the parking lot of Gilles custard stand got used to seeing him conduct baseball's official business while sitting in his car eating lunch.

Bud Selig speaks in Washington DC in July 1994, about two years after he became baseball's acting commissioner. In 1998, he was named permanent commissioner.

OUT OF THE DARKNESS

On August 11, 1994, baseball players walked off their jobs and did not return until the following March. The 1994 season concluded without a World Series for the first time since 1904. "It was tough. There was a lot of anger everywhere, particularly amongst our fans," commissioner Bud Selig recalled.

The owners and players laid the foundation for labor peace and prosperity in 1997. That year, they agreed to a contract that included sharing money among all 30 teams and forcing teams to pay a penalty when their payrolls went above a predetermined amount. Another agreement, one that included random drug testing of players, followed in 2002. Since then, new stadiums have popped up and baseball found a new source of money in fans willing to pay to follow games on computers and cell phones.

to three. Milwaukee moved to the AL Central. But the owners' efforts, led by Selig, to lower the costs of fielding a team caused a strike by the players. This led to Selig canceling the last part of the 1994 season and the postseason.

Major League Baseball and Selig were widely criticized for not being able to solve their problems. It was only just before the 1995 season was to start that the two sides agreed to play again.

Selig faced another big fight in his hometown. His long campaign to replace aging Milwaukee County Stadium with a new stadium that would help the Brewers make more money was approaching a do-or-die point. The Brewers wanted a stadium with a retractable roof.

A vote on October 6, 1995, in the Wisconsin Senate was

Miller Park is shown before the Brewers' first regular-season game there, held on April 6, 2001, against the Reds. Milwaukee won 5–4.

needed to approve a sales tax to fund the proposed ballpark. The vote just passed, 16–15. Plans unfolded for a stadium that would be built next to County Stadium. It would be called Miller Park. This was thanks to a large contribution from the nearby Miller Brewing Co.

But history shows that nothing comes easily for the Brewers. Their plan to open Miller Park for the 2000 season suffered a tragic setback on July 14, 1999. That day, a 467-foot (142-m) crane collapsed while lifting a 450-ton (408-t) piece of steel. Three ironworkers were killed. An estimated $100 million in damage was done to the stadium. Miller Park would not open until 2001.

By the time the Brewers moved into their new digs, they had made more history off the field. They switched leagues. Interleague play had begun in 1997. A more complicated 1998 schedule made it necessary for one AL team to move to the NL. After the Kansas City Royals turned down Selig's offer to switch leagues, he moved his own team to the NL. Part of the reasoning was that the Brewers and the Chicago Cubs were logical geographic rivals. Indeed, games between those teams would prove to result in larger than usual crowds in Milwaukee. The added ticket revenue would benefit the Brewers.

The last order of business needed to make the Brewers successful was finding someone willing to buy the team and operate it with a bigger budget. Selig passed the ownership of the Brewers to daughter Wendy Selig-Prieb when he became permanent commissioner on July 9, 1998. Some critics were not satisfied. They claimed that the commissioner favored the Brewers. The team's 12 straight losing seasons before an 81–81 finish in 2005 helped to quiet some of the complaints.

A California businessman named Mark Attanasio headed a group that bought the Brewers from the Seligs on September 28, 2004. Helping him was that more than a decade of losing had resulted in several high draft picks. Those picks

CC Sabathia delivers a pitch in September 2008. The Brewers' trade for the left-hander that season helped lift them into the playoffs.

were turning into star players for the Brewers.

A slugging team built around Prince Fielder and Ryan Braun brought big crowds to Miller Park. The new standard for a good Brewers season attendance became 3 million.

In 2008, Attanasio and general manager Doug Melvin credited the fans' support for helping them decide to trade several minor league prospects to the Cleveland Indians for star pitcher CC Sabathia on July 7. Sabathia went on to lead

Prince Fielder, *right,* receives congratulations from Milwaukee teammate Ryan Braun after hitting a homer in 2009.

Milwaukee to an NL wild-card berth and its first postseason appearance since 1982.

The final month of that season was tense. The Brewers lost 11 of their first 14 games in September. That cost manager Ned Yost his job. Third-base coach Dale Sveum was promoted to acting manager with 12 games left in the season. The Brewers finished 90–72 and held off the New York Mets for the wild card.

It was on to the NL Division Series (NLDS) against the Philadelphia Phillies. The Brewers lost the first two games on the road. In Game 3, Milwaukee won 4–1 in the first-ever playoff contest at Miller Park. But the Phillies hit four home runs in Game 4 to win 6–2 and take the series three games to one.

The Brewers finally had returned to the postseason. Hope was alive in Milwaukee. The fans returned 3 million strong in 2009. Milwaukee finished 80–82. Two years after smashing an NL-high 50 home runs, Fielder hammered 46. Braun added 32 homers. The Brewers celebrated their 40th season in good shape.

But, as history shows, nothing comes easily for the Brewers. The team did not play very well in 2010, despite the fact that Milwaukee received All-Star seasons from left fielder Braun, right fielder Corey Hart, and pitcher Yovani Gallardo.

The Brewers kept moving on up. The 2011 season brought the teams highest winning percentage ever. They made it to the NLCS and won Game 1, but were eliminated by the St. Louis Cardinals, the eventual World Series champs.

The Brewers put up another winning record in the 2012 season, but not like 2011. And 2013 was worse, with 74 wins and 88 losses.

Though the last two seasons were rough, the Brewers had several talented but still young players, giving fans reason to be optimistic about the future.

The Crusher

In 2007, Brewers first baseman Prince Fielder became the youngest major league player to hit 50 home runs in a season. He was 23 years and 139 days old. Hall of Famer Willie Mays had been the youngest at 24 years, 137 days in 1955. Fielder finished the 2007 season with an even 50, breaking the Brewers' record of 45 shared by Gorman Thomas in 1979 and Richie Sexson in 2001 and 2003.

TIMELINE

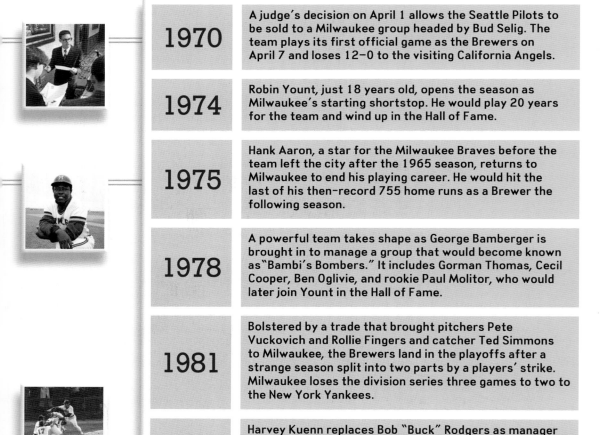

1970 A judge's decision on April 1 allows the Seattle Pilots to be sold to a Milwaukee group headed by Bud Selig. The team plays its first official game as the Brewers on April 7 and loses 12–0 to the visiting California Angels.

1974 Robin Yount, just 18 years old, opens the season as Milwaukee's starting shortstop. He would play 20 years for the team and wind up in the Hall of Fame.

1975 Hank Aaron, a star for the Milwaukee Braves before the team left the city after the 1965 season, returns to Milwaukee to end his playing career. He would hit the last of his then-record 755 home runs as a Brewer the following season.

1978 A powerful team takes shape as George Bamberger is brought in to manage a group that would become known as "Bambi's Bombers." It includes Gorman Thomas, Cecil Cooper, Ben Oglivie, and rookie Paul Molitor, who would later join Yount in the Hall of Fame.

1981 Bolstered by a trade that brought pitchers Pete Vuckovich and Rollie Fingers and catcher Ted Simmons to Milwaukee, the Brewers land in the playoffs after a strange season split into two parts by a players' strike. Milwaukee loses the division series three games to two to the New York Yankees.

1982 Harvey Kuenn replaces Bob "Buck" Rodgers as manager on June 2, and the team dubbed "Harvey's Wallbangers" takes off. The Brewers win the AL East on the final day, outduel the Angels for the AL pennant, then lose a seven-game World Series to the St. Louis Cardinals.

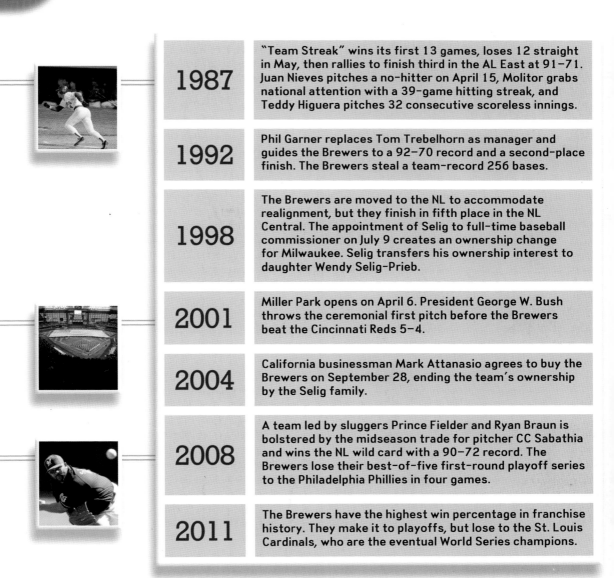

1987 — "Team Streak" wins its first 13 games, loses 12 straight in May, then rallies to finish third in the AL East at 91–71. Juan Nieves pitches a no-hitter on April 15, Molitor grabs national attention with a 39-game hitting streak, and Teddy Higuera pitches 32 consecutive scoreless innings.

1992 — Phil Garner replaces Tom Trebelhorn as manager and guides the Brewers to a 92–70 record and a second-place finish. The Brewers steal a team-record 256 bases.

1998 — The Brewers are moved to the NL to accommodate realignment, but they finish in fifth place in the NL Central. The appointment of Selig to full-time baseball commissioner on July 9 creates an ownership change for Milwaukee. Selig transfers his ownership interest to daughter Wendy Selig-Prieb.

2001 — Miller Park opens on April 6. President George W. Bush throws the ceremonial first pitch before the Brewers beat the Cincinnati Reds 5–4.

2004 — California businessman Mark Attanasio agrees to buy the Brewers on September 28, ending the team's ownership by the Selig family.

2008 — A team led by sluggers Prince Fielder and Ryan Braun is bolstered by the midseason trade for pitcher CC Sabathia and wins the NL wild card with a 90–72 record. The Brewers lose their best-of-five first-round playoff series to the Philadelphia Phillies in four games.

2011 — The Brewers have the highest win percentage in franchise history. They make it to playoffs, but lose to the St. Louis Cardinals, who are the eventual World Series champions.

QUICK STATS

FRANCHISE HISTORY

Seattle Pilots (1969)
Milwaukee Brewers (1970–)

WORLD SERIES

1982

AL CHAMPIONSHIP SERIES
(1969–97)

1982

NL CHAMPIONSHIP SERIES
(1998–)

2011

DIVISION CHAMPIONSHIPS

1981 (second-half title), 1982

KEY PLAYERS
(position[s]; seasons with team)

Hank Aaron (DH; 1975–76)
Ryan Braun (3B/OF; 2007–)
Mike Caldwell (SP; 1977–84)
Cecil Cooper (1B; 1977–87)
Prince Fielder (1B; 2005–2011)
Rollie Fingers (RP; 1981–82,
    1984–85)
Teddy Higuera (SP; 1985–91,
    1993–94)
Paul Molitor (2B/3B/DH; 1978–92)
Ben Oglivie (OF; 1978–86)
George Scott (1B; 1972–76)
Gorman Thomas (OF; 1973–83, 1986)
Pete Vuckovich (SP; 1981–86)
Robin Yount (SS, OF; 1974–93)

KEY MANAGERS

George Bamberger (1978–80,
    1985–86): 377–351
Harvey Kuenn (1982–83):
    160–118; 6–6 (postseason)

HOME PARKS

Sick's Stadium (1969)
Milwaukee County Stadium
    (1970–2000)
Miller Park (2001–)

* All statistics through 2013 season

The Braves were playing their last game in Milwaukee on September 22, 1965, and Bud Selig was walking among the sad patrons at County Stadium. He had formed a group that tried to keep the Braves in the city and, having failed that, would try to find a replacement team. "Somebody tapped me on the back and I turned around, and this older woman was standing there," Selig recalled. "She said, 'You're all we've got now. Don't let us down.'"

The Seattle Pilots had a forgettable 1969 season except for one thing. Pitcher Jim Bouton wrote about what went on behind the scenes in a book called *Ball Four*. It became a bestseller and set new standards of sportswriting.

The Brewers in 1970 had an outfielder who wore No. 44, whose first name was Hank, and whose last name sounded a lot like Aaron over the County Stadium loudspeakers. But Hank Allen was no Hank Aaron—or even Dick Allen, his more famous brother who was a star slugger for several teams. Hank Allen played in only 28 games for Milwaukee and hit .230 with no home runs.

The term "cheesehead" and the foam rubber cheesehead headgear came into vogue during the Brewers' "Team Streak" season of 1987. Ralph Bruno, whose Foamation company makes the distinctive hat, explains: "I was reupholstering my mother's couch when I got the idea. People from Chicago would also call people from Wisconsin 'cheeseheads' in sort of a negative [way]. But I liked cheese, and I figured what's the big deal? So I cut out a piece of the cushion of the couch, burnt some holes in it, and painted it to look like a big slice of cheddar cheese." He said he wore it to a Brewers game, other fans asked how they could get one, and the idea took off from there.

GLOSSARY

baffling

Confusing so as to keep from understanding.

bankrupt

Financially ruined; a company or person who has less money and assets than money owed.

berth

A place, spot, or position, such as in the baseball playoffs.

commissioner

A person authorized to perform certain tasks or endowed with certain powers.

expansion

In sports, to add a franchise or franchises to a league.

free agent

A player whose contract has expired and who is able to sign with a team of his choice.

legendary

Well known and admired over a long period.

leprosy

A skin disease that can be caught by having contact with someone who has it.

postseason

The games in which the best teams play after the regular-season schedule has been completed.

raucous

Loud and rowdy.

retractable

Can be opened or closed mechanically depending on the weather.

veteran

An individual with great experience in a particular endeavor.

FOR MORE INFORMATION

Further Reading

Aaron, Hank, and Lonnie Wheeler. *I Had a Hammer: The Hank Aaron Story*. New York: HarperCollins Publishers, 1991.

Haudricourt, Tom. *Brewers Essential*. Chicago: Triumph Books, 2008.

Uecker, Bob, and Mickey Herskowitz. *Catcher in the Wry*. New York: G. P. Putnam's Sons, 1982.

Websites

To learn more about Inside MLB, visit **booklinks.abdopublishing.com**. These links are routinely monitored and updated to provide the most current information available.

Places to Visit

Maryvale Baseball Park
3600 North 51st Avenue
Phoenix, AZ 85031
623-245-5500
milwaukeebrewers.mlb.com/spring_training/
This has been the Brewers' spring-training ballpark since 1998.

Miller Park
One Brewers Way
Milwaukee, WI 53214
414-902-4400
mlb.mlb.com/mil/ballpark/index.jsp
This has been the Brewers' home field since 2001. The team plays 81 regular-season games here each year. Tours are available when the Brewers are not playing.

National Baseball Hall of Fame and Museum
25 Main Street
Cooperstown, NY 13326
1-888-HALL-OF-FAME
www.baseballhall.org
This hall of fame and museum highlights the greatest players and moments in the history of baseball. Robin Yount, Paul Molitor, and Hank Aaron are among the former Brewers enshrined here.

INDEX

About the Author

Gary Derong is a newspaper copy editor based in St. Paul, Minnesota. He is a native of Milwaukee, Wisconsin, who has followed the Brewers since their inception and also followed the Milwaukee Braves. He dedicates this book to the memory of devout Brewers fan Iain Campbell (1974–2010) of Brookfield and West Allis, Wisconsin.